NAME YOUR BIRD WITHOUT A GUN

NAME YOUR BIRD WITHOUT A GUN
A TAROT ROMANCE-IN-VERSE
BY EMILY CARR

Copyright © 2020 by Emily Carr
All rights reserved.

This book may not be reproduced, in whole or in part, in any form (beyond that copying permitted by Sections 107 and 108 of the U.S. Copyright Law and except by reviewers for the public press), without written permission from the publishers.

Book design by Drew Burk.
Cover design by Richard Siken.

ISBN 978-1-948510-35-6

Spork Press
Tucson, AZ
SPORKPRESS.COM

But the beginning of things, of a world especially, is necessarily
vague, tangled, chaotic, & exceedingly disturbing.
How few of us ever emerge from such beginning!
How many souls perish in its tumult!
~ Kate Chopin

So it was not a desire for pleasure
(the pleasure came as an extra bonus) but for possession
of the world (slitting open the outstretched body of the world
with his scapel) that sent him in pursuit of women.
~ Milan Kundera

You cannot seize, take, contain within yourself such love:
it is so absolutely intended to be passed onward beyond you
& needs you only for the ultimate charge
that will propel its orbit.
~ Rainer Maria Rilke

TABLE OF CONTENTS

ACT I
SPONTANEOUS INNER SPACE
PAGE 3

ACT II
RESURRECTION REFRAINS
PAGE 25

ACT III
BLUEPRINT FOR A HUMAN
PAGE 47

ACT IV
LA FEMME ARMÉE
PAGE 69

ACROBATS OF THE PSYCHIC MISDEMEANOR
PAGE 89

CYCLOPEDIA OF CARD MEANINGS
PAGE 103

INDEX OF KEY WORDS
PAGE 107

ACKNOWLEDGMENTS & REFERENCES
PAGE 117

NAME YOUR BIRD WITHOUT A GUN

I
SPONTANEOUS INNER SPACE

HANGNAIL
THE WORLD, REVERSED

Liberty stands without shadows
on the asphalt at midday—

Now go deeper, she thinks. *To belong is to forget...*
There is hope in the landscape & passion in the children—

The sun bleeds on pale diners behind cellophane—
Oxygen & hydrogen gather to be somewhere else—Coke
& orange float in styrofoam—

A housecat gnaws fine bones—
—*What happened* Liberty thinks, *versus sometimes
what it meant*—

Small butterflies wobble through terrible sweet heat—

Children's voices fall like rain, strung with fingers
of clarity old men on benches fish the Milky Way—

Liberty dreams of redemption but knows better
than that too—

WHAT THE DEAD WOULD LIKE TO DO
BUT IN MOST CASES CAN'T—
ACE OF CUPS, REVERSED

Sunday sets its white fire
in rhinestone. Liberty walks home her legs move bone
to bone. One part of her brain
is controlling her feet while the other drops
off the tree of heaven. Decidedly the husband
will never return—She passes little gardens, clipped
grass, houses like wads of paper, a church
in absent-minded shadow, a blind
curve up a sudden hill. One by one the trees stop
breathing. A shooting star vanishes,

never to be see again by human eyes.
She would like to kill herself but she's told
she must go on, at any cost. Obedient, Liberty
thinks to herself without wonder, to the laws
of meat, like gravity or Christ—
How you postponed this reckoning Liberty thinks
by believing you lacked a desire
to know. Here, while you are
listening to a leaf scrape air, your heart
mudsmeared

TWO PIECES OF YESTERDAY
TWO OF CUPS, REVERSED

Hollereyed the moon tries on gas station, soda
machine, locked toilet, linedried sheets, a caterpillar
fording yard dirt.

A naked buckeye in torn bandage. In one
glass juice, whiskey in another. Photons fall. The radio
talks back. She is crying now, her head thrust, one
hand on her forehead, the bare syllables collecting like
water over her breasts.

He is gone.

(A couplet makes a stab in the dark.)
(The just enough-ness impulse that would keep her breathing.)

The black silhouette of a cat rearranges itself on a road that loses
itself in landscape.

(Why not why.) (Tell the truth or I'll jump.)

Lord Liberty thinks, *it is so easy: to say someone loved you. Pawned himself, limb after. Pulled his spent pronoun through. Light, at his back*

MORNING EXERCISE
PAGE OF CUPS

What you need to know is her coordinates
are elsewhere. She is working with only a few
elements of memory. Two or three scenes. A single landscape.
The desperate arms of corn & star. Abandoned cigarettes.
The housecat, hunting early. Broken
beer bottles scattered over tombstones. A single season: spring.
Belly yellow out of the old Ford the sun swoops
down & scoops up some wet sparrows shaking
their wings in the wind-crazy poplars. *Darling* Liberty prays,
don't think I didn't love you. It's precisely because I love you
that your death has set me free—

THAT PARTICULAR GREEN, NEVER
KNIGHT OF CUPS

Liberty thinks she should. Look
for some sign at least.

Square swift clouds move across the afternoon.

Tornadoes fall down, & drown themselves
in the Mississippi. There is black & there is blue
shadow: this includes
the air in the trees blowing out
over the freeway. Joints of
gospel & a pregnancy test in the dream.

Pretty blooms in the drainage ditch.
The ghost of her turning dark in the grass.

(Fate. Which requires less. Than
volition. It requires only inertia.)

CARTESIAN PROSTHESIS
FIVE OF PENTACLES

At a salon downtown Liberty lies naked on a tanning bed.

She hears d#, the one above middle C. Thick
& tart like rain.

She turns on her back, her left hand makes a fist. She listens
to the radio talking back to the afternoon, lets
the weather report pour through her over the world.

She remembers a peaked house, a flag, straight rows of corn, bright
cut roses in the passenger seat.

In the contrived humidity of the salon in safety
goggles, a hundred days or more from the husband there is no
going back.

In the dirt of her heart: without headlights
the husband is driving quickly. Saucered lights, a pickup
emerges.

She lets her body go loose & the heat seems to draw
down until she is inside it flesh of the world. With a puzzled
certainty she knows now the lie all lovers tell themselves:
we *invented* this—

QUEEN FOR A DAY
FOUR OF WANDS, REVERSED

Brass couplets drift across concrete, succumb to shattered
simile relieved only by the bend of her knee, an elbow
resting on tombstone.

The wings of her hipbones line up without comment, her wet
fingers spoon salt.

She is Cassiopeia, weeping on a day without Gods.

Her husband is dead; or he has disappeared.
He has left no note: he will be met by no one; there is no
one to save him.

Sheet lightning slumbers lightly, ruffles, swells, increases
the trees.

She follows; she walks or is carried a long
way, across sand dunes & then the river swallowing
grass. She was born in July, but now

she feels like January. Alone & unannounced Liberty
is a contraction in the clouds. Down hand over hand from the moon
on a rope. She turns her head & cannot

see the children in the trees. With a blank mind she licks
her fingers. Poor driftwood! Poor bird! Rose
to bone to air in that shrug of star. In caesura yes another

dumb animal making that final leap—

DEATH DOES NOT MEAN DEATH
DEATH, REVERSED

Scattered among some buckeyes at six am at the edge
of a field, Liberty passes a jumble of cannibalized
cars. She pulls over. A doe & her yearly browse, skinny by
pecans breathing Sunday blue.

The energy she thinks, *required to ask the right question? Is so great.*

Like a small frog at the bottom of a fish tank (is it
mine?) she imagines Whitman re-planning his funeral. *The nihilists*
she hears Peabody the narrator saying *say it is the end,
the fundamentalists, the beginning: when in reality it is not more...*
(Nor would death have come had
she not—

Liberty reclines, rolls down the windows. Two dying
sycamores embrace, give way to handpainted signs & roadside
irises: rough tongue, violet exclamation.

Nothing for it Lord she thinks, *between us: nothing.*

*Nothing left of what we really experienced, our thoughts, our
memories, our sensations, from which we are
becoming more & more separated: that reality, which is, simply
my life—*

The sky goes gold behind carnation smear. Faith
dawns blind. It resets. Automatically. To metabolism & panic.
It comes forward. I am only   my
mother

—THE PART OF THE BRAIN
WE SHARE WITH TREX
THE MOON, REVERSED

Crickets wind their one note to the breaking, a lone
squirrel runs guy wire, the subtle slinking cat stands
inside the moon's shadow, which is one hundred
miles wide & travels at two thousand mph.

Dusk falls: useful, ordinary. For one moment in her ignorant
body which is so glad to be alive... Liberty sits by the window &
counts thirty-four crows. Opening a can of wet food,
she imagines herself a bride in the kitchen. The sketchier
the better, like a simply drawn woman pouring
milk from a pitcher.

She puts on a translucent yolky sundress & eats
a communion tablet. *Let me!* she says. *Everyone else has died, why
shouldn't I*

The drug enters the beautiful membranes of her
eyes, lights up one cell at a time until her brain is flooded
with sound or silence. *There are* she thinks *some
desperate oaks in here. Belief, or dream: with its immediate branches.*

In the air she thinks *there are tennis balls & chemical
experiments, there is semen & spit, there is holy words & Audubon's
Oriole, there is false molecules of memory colliding
with the past, there is a marimba in the trees saying
water, water.*

There is what love is there is her bare feet saying
it is over: flat like a dream on both sides she is
the heroine let her do it—

THE LAW OF UNINTENDED CONSEQUENCE
QUEEN OF PENTACLES, REVERSED

That softly repeating plink, distant at first?

The rain's tower rises, & Liberty walks in a huge
cathedral of hearing that has somehow entered her.

Her soul descends into her belly, vibrates like a butterfly
or a few nervous bats.

Marriage she thinks *was not a life already
lived so much as a life that stopped
moving forward into the past.* Night turns

on her blue heel: clean knots of cloud are tied & untied.

Children run screaming as if choreographed
around bright plastic animals, a perfect violin.

Moonstruck thunder pounds on her veins: down through
memory slender up through the drug.

A thunderstorm, lurking in the singed
forest. Witness flung out like a handful of pale doves—

POOM
FIVE OF CUPS

Show me.

(She is crying now.)

Show me.

Poom the sky says.

The shadow of God's hand huge on Liberty's shoulder...
threw grief across the verandah while the world slept.

Meanwhile (to quote Freud): one perfect rose.

Lightning streams through the world like hair...

Cardinals & tomatoes: in a white forked flame.

Scraps of bright trumpet, clean knots of blue
melody, the moon bleeding in dreams of forest—

IN THE TIME OF COMBINES & LUCK
SEVEN OF PENTACLES

(The sun cracks the horizon of a red phrase.)

(Blue jays fly from torn signature. Ants & sycamores go on eating air.)

(The husband stands there: green, next
to the ruins.) (In his footsteps rose,

& a drop of blue salt.) (Deaf lilies; shattered cells
of thunderhead.)

Liberty sits across from an empty cathedral. Grief pours from her sundressed arms like smoke.

There is she thinks, *no story in which your failure is not background—*

NEW = SOME
SEVEN OF CUPS

This is the second time Liberty almost died.
She remembers: beautiful birds trying

on the trees, chlorophyll vibrating on the edge of green
death, silver apology, June bugs forsaken

on the sidewalk at noon.
Angels scavenge her empty veins, fat bars

of sunlight fall across her face. God is breathing
her back she returns rainwashed

& windstripped. Inside her mind the sunlight
is like knives. *Get out*

of my dream Liberty says *get*   *out*

FLIPOVER
TEMPERANCE

On the sixth day she wakes: like a pre-Raphaelite angel
aloft on leather wings.

Her stomach is hard & flat, beyond reproach.
She has a terrible thirst. Grocery wine. Wonderbread.

Kool-Aid. Fruit loops. Her mind repeats arrivals, instructions,
departures, the white voices

of the refrigerator. She arranges poppies in a silver vase
on the windowsill. Pockets

a penny from the threshold's spine. Across
her grief she writes left to right: *go on: finish*

those years that might have belonged   to someone else—

A PAGE STRAIGHT FROM GOD'S PLAN
EIGHT OF WANDS, REVERSED

Liberty hangs laundry briskly shaken
between buckeyes. Knocks half inches of strawberry wine cooler
back like whiskey. Knowing it won't do any
good carves his initials
in buckeye. *Like Midas* she thinks, *touching
his daughter, roses, servants, the water in a fountain*—Liberty lies
with the Bible on her stomach & falls
asleep with all the lights on.

ALL THE HIGHWAYS END IN SKY
QUEEN OF CUPS

The coffin was lowered. The earth goes on caressing
his satin parts especially. Liberty eats some aspirin, lights
a cigarette.

In her heart is faded *f*s, a downy *s*, the syllables sift
the husband through. Spring snow falls shyly.

The plot staggers away, approaches the left margin, lays low, purrs.

(Once, she was so young!)

(Once she would give up nothing.)

Great globs of hemoglobin fall redly, make sonatas
with stones, the western ruin of sky turns, & in that fine bright
suspension before Christ moves in its halo—

It's just a memory Liberty tells herself, *you can change it*

IT COULD NO LONGER BE METAPHORIC
KING OF CUPS

It is summer or the end of summer or some other deceitful
season. In an expensive place in the middle of a loud song Liberty
is alone drinking

French wine, eavesdropping on some housewives.
It's been two months. I knew them.
It's terrible. No trace. None. It was on TV.
Was it murder?
They looked everywhere.
Kidnapping?
Who would do that?
They showed her on TV, his wife. It was heartbreaking.
Liberty is listening sullen in a phoenix
dress with bugle beads, her dark hair twisted in braids.

You sit down next to her, light a cigarette, put
it out, order whiskey, assume

a lionhearted posture in your fur coat. Liberty lays
her knife & fork across the white plate, tucks
her dress around her thighs.

Now she is speaking: in the language of fish.
Her eyes are blue, unwashed. Light meatless addicted—all
her pronouns shift. Her hands making
simple gestures. Mingled with shyness it
drives you half-wild. You cross out all your syllables, the sun
bends her knees, a pitcher winds
up, some peaches grow inside the trees.
In the delirium of a summer afternoon. The affair begins.

A RESCUE STORY
THE EMPEROR

It's the day after Labor Day.

Liberty is burning letters in a carless lot. The wind going
backwards, retracing her steps

in the third person. Rain hunts
silence, makes rivers of her bare feet. Cicada sex

& birdsong blow white against her thighs. Silent
lightning leaps across the sky, thunder

makes the great dayending sound of heartbreak.
She is a drowned Ophelia, you

a lanky Antony.

If you are going to do this she tells herself, *do not
be embarrassed. Do not skip the difficult parts. Do not be*

embarrassed.

PAPERING OVER THE WALTZ IN HER LIFE
KING OF PENTACLES

A comet trespasses over a crater.

Developments pan out & blacktop confronts
the pasture. Overgrowth & abandoned farm implements hem
in your exhaust counters, the frame of corn & tree recedes.

A telephone pole gets repeated, & is music. Tucked
in your pocket Liberty's pulse is giving off soft dactyls.

Everyone's love you say, *has a problem. What's* yours.

(You're very good at lying Liberty thinks.) (*Do I sound
like a liar?*) (*You sound like you enjoy lying*

to women.)

At the edge of a field that cuts the road
in two a cow is eating cut grass cured for fodder & witnessing
the sky.

Some people Liberty says, *want to lift you up, & some are like
crawdads, they just want to drag you down.*

She is cross section of a girl. (Just a scale
somewhere, a phrase hearing herself   think

DOSTOEVSKY'S IDIOT
TEN OF CUPS

Seven o'clock & already it's impossible to understand the presence
of the sky, or of trees. (When yesterday Liberty woke & suddenly
can live or die without fear. How

to convey that sense.) (She'd almost forgotten.)

The sun sets herself down in merciful pieces.

The grasses make simple gestures, she throws her body against
yours, with intuitive thrusts of hope & rib.

Which is to say: without a clear aim
in mind. The angel raises its arrow. Her soul shuffles, leaving
a bright scrape: like the hinges of dream (in the middle

of things.) A cloud flings the moon over her buttocks.
(Or did it? You were   there; you ought
to know

II
RESURRECTION REFRAINS

—THE INFINITE ZERO NOTHING FITS INTO—
THE FOOL

It is raining a little, & morning. You kiss her
without blinking.

Tell me Liberty says *your story.*

There is none.

What we remember you say *is only our own listening.*

She lifts her beautiful braceleted arm, combs
your hair. Her eyes are blue, & change all the time.

Day to day Liberty says *we are living in a fiction, in
a narrative, in order to do away with the ambiguity—*

You imagine her longlegged in the middle
distance: like Archimedes in the Kansas light, full of hyperbole,
hope & promise, a clumsy brightness drinking

sun, wetfurred & mudslung. (Surely, it is all wrong—

I can't you say, *say for sure I'll always*

LATERAL GENE EXCHANGE
ACE OF WANDS

Liberty puts her wedding ring in a Band-Aid box, her sundress flowers sideways.

Sin & shadow run over the flat heaven of her belly combing your limbs.

Cattails ripple, fatten. Somewhere, the desperate sound of crickets greasing their pronouns.

Her hunger breaks. Zero at the bone.

All distance, all breath.

Inside that startled space, your hands like hot salt. *Jesus* she cries. *How does a body do—*

She is becoming someone else: not the person she wanted to be. Like Madame Bovary sitting down with a pen & the notion of Flaubert, *c'est moi*

PATHETIC CRUSOE
PAGE OF WANDS

Her silhouette gathers up hair, her breasts drop
their fruit, a nipple shines through. *Stop* you think, *stop right
there.*

This isn't you think, *what I was asking for this isn't, what
I was asking for.*

But already in four o'clock delirium she
undresses completely & for the first time you see her naked.

Her ribs bare as she pulls the tee over her head, hips curving
as she removes her panties.

It's four o'clock the crickets are greasing their pronouns,
a few nervous bats leap at coyote nocturnes. Liberty
counts back from ten,

you run your fingers along the line between tanned & virgin.
Nothing but nothing could have stopped you—

HEAVEN CAN WAIT
THE LOVERS

When you have survived
the terror of the first night together, when
she has held your hand while you sleep when in the wordless
hot silence your conscience unwinds—

The planet tilts; the day before yesterday goes zinc.

Holy & beautiful she says, *as seen from inside surrender—*

You are unarranged. *Absolutely I can* you think.

The first time I loved she says, *it was an accident.*
The second time it hurt like hell.
The third time I meant she says, *to last it out. Not* she says,
regretting how I came a fourth time to—

Your fingers make bootheel halfmoons, you count
the ribs you will carry along & the ribs you will have
to leave behind. Liberty is wearing a see-through negligee.

She is lighting the bathroom with candles & sprinkling
potpourri & spearmint in steaming water.
Flushed, on tiptoe.

Watch her rounded & scooped by electrons falling
the sky opening like gills like flowers become flesh. (In retrospect,
you can: forgive yourself for everything—

30

—QUOTIDIAN PAROLE
THE DEVIL

It is pitiless downpouring sunset sitting skinny on the edge
of punctuated scripture. It is the day before

yesterday. You are waiting in a leatherette booth painted
the color of a swimming pool.

In an orange dress with lacy gray panties, Liberty shows
you her tattoos: blue sequins, initials, a Eucharist stripe
across the idea of heaven.

Like blades she deals her pretty words (how
brilliant). You slip one hand up her thigh. Some of her molecules rub
off on yours. Her eyes pivot over a spoon. *Love*

she says, *being a Euclidian triangle & suicide the restless
calculus of its curve*—You put

your hand there. She is at her most
delicate & polluted you are ready to dare anything this is how
you like it. There is music, or the empty

molecules between. On the leaf
of a plate: fluted bones. Applesauce & flank steak.

She drinks Wild Turkey, you drink Pabst. In the white
voices of the air conditioner all her memories: terribly
leaked. One wrong move is all it takes.

It is the seventy-two-hour anniversary
of your affair. (Anniversary, as in the tacit agreement you made
from the start. It keeps its word.

"ISIS UNVEILED"
THE HIGH PRIESTESS, REVERSED

One: you are sure it is love.
(But what is betrayal? Breaking ranks & going off
into the unknown.)

(In this moment Liberty knows who she is: a traitor.)
(For if it's the rest of us who are killed
by the suicide, it's herself whom the mistress kills, only
she has to do it over, & over, & over.)

Two: you are sure love is incompatible
to living in the long run. Such things happen in the story, they do not
happen in the world.

(I don't know why but you feel it happening.)
(When no one's looking touch her.)

(But isn't it enough to love.) (Isn't it enough to go on
living.) (Just what   in your heart did you want
to happen.)

The music stops, & a child's voice breaks
over the lonely parking lot. Cattails ripple, fatten. Leaves go on,
with the grass being green.

It is not like fate but rather
as if reality had disappeared. (Despair kept,

they say, Goethe going, who sat under a tree often
in the center of it all before it happened.)

Three: but there is no three   to what you know.

"SQUARING THE CIRCLE"
TWO OF WANDS

Hydrogen & oxygen fall through trees.
Fat clouds & strange lightbulbs.
Fish shaped like tattered stars. Iridescent bacteria
in the sediment of letters.

Cumulus boil. Churchbells come again in wet speech.

On a wooden deck over water.
Liberty is some kind of beautiful accident like wild
lilacs smoldering in the short grass.

Rilke's angels dangle from her ears. In lip gloss, no
bra & a blue dress with finches she is reading
the lives of the saints: dying

men pierced by arrows & women staring at the white
leopards of heaven as flames lick their breasts.
She likes the ornately lettered names, the early

paragraphs yawning with martyrs, waiting
to be tempted.

Listen: choice matters exactly
as much as it doesn't. (Why? I don't know but you
feel it happening.

There is no death like this except (if you remember it)
your baptism

HOPES & FEARS
THREE OF PENTACLES

At a picnic table in Blue Heaven next to the Church
of the God of the Prophecy you drink rum punch & eat
Angels on horseback.

The waitress is pale, shy. A heartless soloist flies
from her mouth. Like churchnoise, that distant animal
echo: *joyful joyful we*

Enormous lightning leaps across the sky. The black trees
seem to beg & shift—

You have let things pass, too much.

Like a red chicken: jerking over corn kernels in the sand.

I mean: a wiser man would understand the flight
of the mistress into a heaven that loves her: like a knife,
separating left from right, redeemed from

unredeemed.

You drink.

You pass through that doorway; you turn the corner.

(Hush.) (Again.)
(Hush.) Please God.)

*One wants you think to create a bright new future. One wants
to create it. Why shouldn't you*

FACTS SEWN WITH STARS
THREE OF WANDS

(Did you not know, then, that love is a terror
whose outcome we don't fear.

We go through the terror from beginning to end, & that
precisely is love at first sight.

(A terror about which you know more
than the beginning.) (A terror in which

you have confidence.)

There are crickets. There is corn hemmed in by corn.
Eggs hatched by the wind. The area (calculus) under the little torch
of a love letter. Gravity: a future you must overcome.

(Does it feel like that.) (Absolutely.)

(Earth to cloud, girl to bird. A blue halo, leaving
a clear space above...

Liberty moves in it: as a fish.)

EASY DOES IT
SEVEN OF WANDS

In my plan to be myself Liberty
says, *I became someone else.* Her earrings swing
over the abysses of slender tulips.

You are in a cafe on the water. The sun shimmies
up the shin of a ditch. Dogwoods fishtail, an exhausted
cloud sheds pale oxygen.

Like the frog she says *made beautiful on its own
amphibian terms.* She uncrosses, re-crosses

her legs. (Yes, as the sea watched Icarus fly
off a tree.) Just to you she speaks this way.

From above & to the right, watching herself as only
another could have—or God.

On her menu you draw Noah's ark in black
& white, thinking *the boat inside the ribs of which a remnant
of terrestrial life could   survive.*

To be seen as a wife did not Liberty says, *make me feel like one—*

It is as if her marriage hadn't quite happened
to her but nearby: like car accidents, or rain. *The terrifying thing*

she says *is that it is done—not what   you've done
but that it is over.*

BETE NOIRE
EIGHT OF CUPS, REVERSED

Cornfields & passions cast their shadows. The sun goes
on: defining the night.

On the kitchen table: broken sandwiches & soft hills
of salt. A paper napkin crumpled

in water spilt through the blades of leaves.

You put dandelions in a Brillo box, draw a tattoo
with tulips. *We were very often drunk* Liberty says,

*because we had no helpful method of perceiving
the world & our positions in it.*

A cloud flexes her bicep imitating

the dogwood next door. Walking with the sky
beneath her feet Liberty serves some spaghetti,

sits down with a big library book. *When people*

are ready to you say, *they change. Sometimes*   *they die before*
they can get around to it.

"SHOW ME THE READING YOU GAVE GOD"—
THE HERMIT, REVERSED

Chrysanthemums of exhaust.
Petroleum & orange rainbows.

Through the gilded ribs of a Ferris wheel. Hanging
like a leaf. Her heart falls on sand; her heart
falls on dinosaur bones.

One thing Liberty knows for sure: love gets done (though
she sometimes has the feeling of being subjected & trying
to name it for the meanwhile.

(That familiar sense of forgetfully—)
(Perhaps by chance.)
(Perhaps, God knows. The husband *had* to vanish. Can't
you understand.

Travel with her, until his death has disappeared—)

A child mounts a tricycle & rides
away into a tree. A blue jay screams on the edge
of virgin cornfield.

Your conscience flashes wildly, like a fish. *Is this*

you think, *normal. There's no way*   *to tell.*

(You are the end of something, are
you not.) (You are nowhere, exactly. Yet the impulse persists—

CONSTITUTIONAL BAGATELLE
QUEEN OF WANDS, REVERSED

Through dramatic climax of wet window the wind
says *hunh*. Dogs of early evening squabble. The ragged
pulse of church bells is pulled into sky.

Liberty unbundles her ribs, sheds her bark & shines.
Tender: cunningly. Make love. (*Make me.*)

Brake lights flower, helicopters lament. Her thighs
happen. Uninvited, they arrive.

(In honor of a beauty that owes us nothing.) A lacy bra
with violent flowers. The melody running away
with your wrists. A cathedral making tribute

to that which does not exist. Like snowflakes falling inside
the globe of Mozart's holy heaven.

(Why did God make us love?) (Because God
loves stories. Peopling the sky with his fish.)

(If one loves, then immediately
one also *admires, fears & defends*.) (So much for love!)

(At some point you will have to admit you have passed
the point of no return, you are hurtling towards a future even
Liberty can't imagine & all around you your intent
runs backwards, grace notes falling off to rendezvous
with her faith or trust or is that word sex

THE MOUNTEBANK & THE MAGUS
THE MAGICIAN

It's tomorrow. Stars fall
through satellites. The music of existential
metaphor, silent songs.
Tears & mute curses. Red
branches poking out of milky sky. Liberty
holds a silver fork, in that sugar

cube muscle twitch in the augury
of heartache. *A piece of space
you say, makes contact with a piece
of time & because they are in constant
motion, you can make the two
one.* You sharpen your pencil,

make a few slashes on a napkin.
A balloon slumps in the corner of the kitchen
like jelly. Liberty sweeps onion
skins, beats an egg. Fixes
catfish. Her wrists are freckled & make
transparent gestures: like a child.

It's two o'clock. It's Tuesday.
It's June. A perfect violin issues from
the radio. On the clock face there are hands
cancelling hands. You try to imagine
the future as you would like it
to be—this heartbreaking beauty, the saving

core of reality, that will
go on, when there is no heart left to break for it—

MESSIAH ON PAROLE
NINE OF WANDS, REVERSED

Chihuahuas ruin the sidewalk, pee on oak leaves.
Girl scouts share secrets on the asphalt.

The truth hums, the truth trembles.
The truth holds.

(What do you want you ought to make up your mind.)
(Or do you believe Liberty has no plot, even this
was taken from her, as all lies are...

She is drinking pink champagne from a thermos
with a logo that looks like a dreamcatcher inside the belly
of a crow. She is looking

for permission: to arrange her limbs easily, in
the orchestration of salaries, weddings & garages. This shouldn't
be a problem but it is.

There is for example what is unforgivable & what
comes after. Small mammals fighting

in the sky. Tiny & expensive, dusk

begins to stretch through the trees. It is as if
you have stepped sideways into a dimension where desire never stops
its course, where, having come to this predicament,

there is only the uncertainty   of all purpose—

REPRODUCTIVE PHYSICS
KING OF WANDS

Beside her you're awake. Your mind turns on itself, in black
fishlike rain.

You run your fingers over that pale seal branded
across her wrists for the love of a distant & different man who
disappeared. *I need* you think, *the truth*

& some aspirin. You take her hand light & cold
go running through your limbs. The moon squeezes herself

through gargoyle clouds, the echo of someone else's
television. From the inside out:
pretend. There is no story yet. Only raw elements.

You had cheated. You   would cheat.
After this, a happy ending seems unnecessary—

THE FIRST OF HER TWELVE LABORS
JUSTICE

Sun fills the gin from the big window behind the sink.
Window shards & cut apart trees. Abraham Lincoln

on a hand towel. Liberty is wearing a necklace made of turquoise
& pendant earrings. Her wrists are wrapped

in Saran. She is dangerous to herself, & in love. Smashing
ice cubes with a wooden spoon. Handsewing

a river out of sequins. Sawing the plastic bracelet
with a grapefruit knife. She is unlacing her shoes, just

in case. Already she can't remember the husband. She
will tell herself this, at any rate. She will rise from the earth
like an animal, & she will go—

IF YOU WANT TO KNOW THE TRUTH
NINE OF CUPS

You order spaghetti & white beer.
Liberty orders coffee, eats some of yours with a spoon.
Is it you or is it she says *us.*

It's us.

Liberty gathers up her hair from falling. Picks at the hems of cold cheese toast on your Fiestaware plate.

Like a duet in which there is no dominant gesture...
(Try not to fall in love.) (It takes everything you have.)

Ok.

Ok.

She orders Whoopie Pie, eats with knife & fork.
Why not.
It takes forever.

It's a bad idea. Ok.
Ok.

(Something there. Something like fate underneath
the words.) (A raked halo almost.) (Now you are the husband's
rival.) (—Something heartless torn from you: like laughter

A CATASTROPHE OF COUPLETS
JUDGMENT, REVERSED

(Tomorrow you will set her free. Tomorrow,
you will let her suffer.)

I admit I am aware of this. *You had to do it—*
You had no idea why—

HOSANNAH
TEN OF WANDS

You have had your go at love & now she is gentle distant
& dreaming backwards.

With its tiny hand & charred heart, the clock hums: two
thirty. Did I? Did I?

Your hand slips a warm shadow across her beautiful
hair, small high buttocks, thighs.

Without their violins cicadas head for the woods little
bracelets of fact   practice *yes, no*.

You never asked would she; Liberty never said she would.

Birds fly across her exposed chest & down one arm:
a black decrescendo. The housecat, wordless, looks up & sees
through you.

Don't trust anybody you never have you never will.

This would make a good ending you think. But
you go on living, of course.

III
BLUEPRINT FOR A HUMAN

REPEAT/NO REPEAT
THE TOWER

October opens into a forest-shaped dream.
The wind gusts, hurtling a dogwood against the fence.

Poom. Christ walks out; the windows keep opening
in her mind. Liberty eats leftover potluck or sheetcake.

You take out an envelope. Draw the snap
of tulip across dirt, a broken sonata, something

burnt. Speak in the direction of her bare shoulder.
My girlfriend you say—

Never she says.

Her voice is like cut roses, gasoline serpents, prompt
little angels in the black glass of fairytale. Her eyes keeping silence
on your chest...

To tell her would break you say, *some rule—*

The word sees you for what you are Liberty, says *without   my help—*

WATCH OUT FOR YOUR FILM MIND
ACE OF SWORDS, REVERSED

You are up on a scaffolding, alone with your conscience,
playing a complex game of proximity & distance. Repeats
arrivals, instructions, departures. Departures. Panic,

though taking its time, will arrive—

Electricity returns to exact its revenge with the white legs
of thunder. Independent of morality

or consequence—
Jumps: your skin swims out
to the limit of sound. You think angels then owls then

semis, lost aeroplanes in the stratosphere. Liberty is gone
your affair never was & here you are, all your resolute molecules
dissolving—

(You are here: of course you are. Wrongsideout:
having sinned.

LIGHT MEAT
TWO OF PENTACLES, REVERSED

Dinner is cooking beautifully away.
Through her heart, which she keeps open: did you think it'd be waltz
come let's   waltz.

... a television, half in the dark facing July.

She is cooking: lilies, or eggs hatched by the wind.
She wants to take a little revenge, & sometimes to make clear
that revenge is not what she is seeking.

She had never been capable, nor wished to be:
of plain honesty. She stares at you over spring onions & makes
no sign.

Short thunder pounds on the windows.
Buckeyes spread every hour to be born away into Venetian.

Standing there halfnaked you know you
possess almost nothing: position. One of the housecats:
spills over, leaves.

1/2 KILO
THREE OF SWORDS

(Which is more demanding—deception of others or self deception?)

(What was she thinking when she fell silent.) (Do you think she will forgive you.)

(Period or question mark?) (If not   you then who.)

"THE BARE RESUME"
FOUR OF SWORDS

You are tired, you can't sleep, you go to the window.

You imagine a closeup black & white closeup of halfnaked
Liberty it drapes & undrapes your silhouette, uselessly giving rise
to what is real—

A minor chord. Smashed against the left elbow of dream.

Whether you are in rapture or in remorse—or is it love?—
you cannot tell. There is no time to consider or to turn
back, or to think of turning.

The hung world gathers: miraculous hatched birds, trees
breathing the shadows back, stars falling in day's collarbone, a fawn
unbandaging while angels wash their underwear
in the miss-ee-ssippi.

What sacrifice: do you think is necessary in the endeavor to become

yourself. You stand over Liberty, you touch her
shoulder, the little curtain of flesh running from belly
to breast. You imagine yourself passing through her thoughts:

a sleepwalker, saying & doing things you would be incapable
of should they occur—

OUR NON-EUCLIDIAN FUTURES
FIVE OF SWORDS

Liberty is eating peaches off a bath towel on the hood
of a black Oldsmobile. There are abandoned

farm implements & chickens taking tiny steps
on flexible knees. Blue shadows turning from stag

at the edge of interstate. *Am I alien to myself*
Liberty thinks, *or only now am I myself: this other*

woman, this irresponsible indecent other woman, of whom
I am jealous, this woman without a destiny who differs
on the surface from other women, but deep down is the same:
full of secret misgivings & fits of jealousy.

Like a fugitive sparrow: unable to fly, or land.

Is it that we aspire to forget the stories we already know.
Or do we learn to forget.

TALK IT OVER WITH LIKEMINDED PEOPLE, YOU NEVER KNOW
SEVEN OF SWORDS

You lean against the crenellations of the air conditioner.
Dandelions migrate in the bellies of beetles.

In flipflops a watch with a sunset
& a palm tree Liberty answers the telephone says *I*, attempts
to find a more convenient form.

Her voice is like a carnation sucking water, sucking
blue. She drinks. *Yes* she says.

The dream she says, *has different beginnings but always
the same end. Someone was going to get hurt—*

She hangs up she turns to you. *Don't* she says, *you dare*

MEMO: BE SMALL
PAGE OF SWORDS

Like the first man & woman naked in each other's trembling presence—there is no simple way to confront the persons you are not...

"ACTION WITHOUT EGO"
STRENGTH, REVERSED

The buckeyes lean back, a white moth kicks up
from her green shoes.

Brake lights make torn whispers. Liberty knows it now &
doesn't know what to do with it & doesn't know what
to do with herself, either.

Sunflowers happen. Uninvited, they arrive.
A river runs away with the field.

The sparrow refuses supper to a sinner in the corn.

As planets & protons invent themselves by spinning,
between you now there is something more

than love: complicity.

HEAVEN CAN WAIT
EIGHT OF PENTACLES

Liberty plays two d#'s on the piano, listens
for the first sparrow. You part her dark hair, your crazy fingers

link. You imagine your love as simpler, more content:
you feed her cake & Coca-Cola.

You point out trees looking like chickens. Get down
on the rug, color or play dominoes. You chew a toothpick:

toss it. Liberty plays a scale like rhymed couplets nude
in a haystack or angels lap-swimming. The air conditioner squanders

the broken notes across your head, shoulders, feet.
You jot a few trees upsidedown in the bone margin.

The black boot, a ring finger, the golden mouths of corpses.
You practice with snowflakes, with Valentines.

Helicopters low over the corn. An exiled patch of sunshine
sliding from her orange dress one wrist to the next.

Can you Liberty says, *change your body or
anything. Anything at all. Everybody seems ok*   *with that
bargain.*

FRANKLIN'S BELOVED MONDAY
HANGED MAN, REVERSED

It's a new day, full of promises you can't keep, or are choosing not to be able...

DOUBTS NOT ONLY ABOUT WHAT TO TELL BUT ABOUT THE VALIDITY OF TELLING AT ALL
EIGHT OF SWORDS

What you need Liberty says, *to know*—

She's not you say, *I didn't want* you say—

Liberty looks, you might think: waterproof, shatterproof, proof.

A one-hundred-pound novel (& very close to diamond)

You take a closeup of her buttocks like little angels below the polka-dot bikini.

I'm not you say, *I never dreamt* you say.

You must have known—

Now & again she looks down at you. Now & again her chin cocks left & a flicker of a smile crosses her face.

Well for one thing you say, *who really was the victim here*—

A SYNCOPATED HALLUCINATION
PAGE OF PENTACLES, REVERSED

The violins hold a high fermata, release.

Seraphim fall like hawks. Liberty has another drink
from the Styrofoam cup.

Perhaps Liberty writes on your greasestained napkin
understanding is.

In a sort of skyblue dress—that shows her shoulders.

You lay your knife & fork across the white plate. You let
yourself down hand over hand, your heart

moves towards her cautiously, unsolved.

A bird is singing. The sun is somewhere down a gong
in the bushes. A cloud flings her skirt over a couple of kites
in competition.

For example Liberty says, *for how much of your life have you
regretted the decisions that saved you?*

Well you think, *you wanted this. If you concentrate
you can make   yourself believe—*

EVERYTHING INTERESTING HAPPENS ON THE MOLECULAR LEVEL
KNIGHT OF SWORDS

Next to you Liberty lays murderously (bad tonight
bad last night & possibly bad again tomorrow). In her pink
thong she is consistent with the formula:
warm blood, no gills, two pairs of hands & a few hairs.

With a constellation of freckles on the nape of her neck & thin
wisps of dream. The moon rises into camera range, a black
silhouette of cat loses itself across the windowsill.

You fuck: dreamy, underwater. Blood seeps
between your loins. All your tendons tremolo. The past
is redeemed, you are forgiven—

STRAIGHT NO CHASER
KNIGHT OF WANDS, REVERSED

Picture Liberty spinning so fast that (like the blades
of an electric fan) her arms disappear.

Every story has a tense, it must take place in time.

Yet there are ways to elide these laws. Neither of you

for example knows the complete truth. Only
one of you knows a section, one of you another: but

to the whole picture only I am invited.

IT COULD NO LONGER BE METAPHORIC
WHEEL OF FORTUNE, REVERSED

You fucked in the country then. But you were both
from somewhere else.

You ride a Ferris wheel you love it for circumference.

Liberty leans back against the stereophonic prairie she is
a negative angel. *Like* Liberty says, *the desert wolf*

who lost his wife & went to the land of the dead for her...

Piped-in music falls over pixels of tree, an insect choir
turns on Vaseline clouds wave bye goodbye

peeling miraculous bow ties of sky.
In her thin dress all shot in red all her molecules seem to fly

open, spread upsidedown across all that darkening
grass. (She really is beautiful, &, remarkably, maybe totally

oblivious to this fact.) (Whereas the weak noise
in your ribs—

Yes; no; yes?
God knows why) (Because you are afraid

Liberty falls through the neon loops into emptiness, alone

YES NO NO YES
NINE OF SWORDS

All day you carry on the experience of the television.

There are pretty girls drinking large daiquiris, a yellow dog
next to a blonde woman with a big hat, laughter vaulting

over the windowsill on its way to the sun. *The question
isn't* Liberty says, *how to get better [you*

won't]. I'm learning she says, *to be ok
with that.* Your shadow turns, clockwise: ripped from your fists.

I don't Liberty says, *want to forget if it
was bad.* Already she is part of your story—straightening

her skirt her flat belly drawing the light in smoke
where the horizon wipes her forehead. You wanted her to love

you; she says so, why not believe her?

SOUVENIR VESPER
KNIGHT OF PENTACLES, REVERSED

The sun falls down then picks
herself up, lies hopelessly starry-eyed amongst
the Queen Anne's Lace.

There is no heat yet. No mosquitoes. No sickening doves.

Just a few gnats warming up, sugaring the asphalt.
The faint shadows of the lighteating leaves falling over

the earth's satin parts especially.

You try to tell yourself the heart is a lie, that the mind
tells the muscle atom upon atom.

You roll away from Liberty. You watch her breathe or not
breathe. (You've come this far so why not—

THE EXTRACTION OF THE SQUARE ROOT
EMPRESS

(Behind that clump of memory that holds the clouds up.)

How any story finally is about the lengths the mind
will carry it to, to explain what the body already knows

RULES FOR DREAMING
TEN OF SWORDS, REVERSED

Liberty is trying to tell herself what she must
have known before in a form she wouldn't recognize
at first. Her body fell in a ditch & lay there

for a while. Rain fringes her face: it talks back. It dips
the trees in grease. A piano cries out
to the blue moon & the stars collect their ghosts.

Who am I Liberty thinks, *if I say*
what I sometimes   mean.

It is an optimism tethered to guilt, & an
intrinsic lack   of self-worth.

Like so. Shiverlet in-slip.
Think of better outcomes. *Be specific* Liberty thinks
how so

IV
LA FEMME ARMÉE

FELO-DE-SE
CHARIOT, REVERSED

I can only imagine how hard it must be for you   to
believe me.

I mean, to hold blame.

I mean, to be you.

I was you   once. I was paradise.

High on a religious hill in the Midwest the sun
recedes until there is nothing. Only the Big Dipper, turning
her incapacities in.

Liberty walks as if she were a dream & didn't know who
was dreaming her.

She comes neatly up to despair right   up to it.

You throw your ball at the wall & catch it again. You
are not sorry that is someone you never learned how to be.

QUOTIDIAN PAROLE
ACE OF PENTACLES, REVERSED

Does the affair continue. Because.
You would change him. Or because.
You were made for him. Or because of.
Future possibility. Or because.
There is no cause.

ICARUS WING MECHANISM AEROSTAT
QUEEN OF SWORDS

The fourth of July begins with a terrific roar of shotguns.

There are cling peaches & cigarettes, fireworks & ham, chicken
eggs in a sand bucket.

A sparrow sings three notes, issues instructions
to tornadoes, rain clouds, grasshoppers. An injured earthworm
drags herself down the sidewalk.

Day gathers in her collarbones, her arteries open
their throats.

What did you hope for after death you say.

It is like Liberty says, *being in love. The desire was there all along
it is born not made—*

TIME STANDS IN PIECES LIKE A FOREST TO BE CHOPPED
TWO OF SWORDS

The drug makes little marathons in her veins.

Soul lands like a paper airplane in the damp violets.

Once Liberty says *someone invented happiness, like the angel's light hands or the hero's paperthin ego. Hormones*

& the will of God—

A ribbon she says. *A leaf—*

We had evolved. A child had died.

This was in real time. A fish is sailing out of sight, & will not close its eyes.

Her skirt hitches, neon shines through.

Piecemeal, & in the third person.

Bronze fibula, a match. Her bright
tattoos, & in nanoseconds.

You know what I'm saying. Somehow you should let
her go—

GOD'S PUNISHMENT, NO PROBABLY NOT
STAR, REVERSED

Eggplants shine on garlic skins. Romaine fills the sink.
Meats drip. All Liberty's ribs go the wrong way.

Night arrives. Pile up food. Pour wine & say miraculous
things. Sit on the floor & wait. Sip.

Wipe your mouth. Pick up cup plate & odd bits of food.
Line the bottles by the door.

On the television at large there are occurrences. The future
as pure leap: that has no end in sight.

In this moment you feel everything is clear. You can take
the loose ends & put them together perfectly, all

the details sum up & you know the ending...
The poppy edges where even the brave—how would you

say—have no windows.

HEAVENLY APPARATUS
THREE OF CUPS, REVERSED

Let us be clear: I am telling only one story & I am telling it on a good day.

Liberty is *in love*; you stand *in front of your love*.

Thinking I have my reasons. (Who are we.) (We are not.)

But the truth is: there are three exits (more   than enough.)

ANGEL VARIATIONS IN AIR PRESSURE
FOUR OF CUPS

The Devil cruises the block in his shiny car, singing—

You say *look*. You say *see*.
You eat ribs & salad from large china plates.
What do you want to be you say. *That's all.*

You do not sit close to one another, you leave plenty
of room between you for the understanding worked out
amidst sheets, television static & cheap Chablis—

When, the Devil croons, *you are human & alone*—

UNINTERESTED COWBOYS
FOUR OF PENTACLES

Hot trees stretch across the sun-drunk horizon.
The television is faraway & spilling
color: powdered sweating men & women with floating
breasts. Silted up trees. Clouds rucked up

over dirt. You drink scotch, hold her hands, kiss
her forehead. She is "on the telephone." She is "at the beach."
She is "sad"; "afraid;" "jealous;" "fatigued."
She is "in orbit." A page straight   from God's book.

You have another drink. It does no good.
It lays anonymous & hard inside you.

The Indians arrive on spotted ponies, whooping.
Their voices tremble on the sundrunk horizon.
With an identical gesture of breasts & arms the beautiful
women scream. Cowboys shoot bright

pistols. The television is full of figures suspended
mid-flight. Liberty breaths, stirs sometimes,
on the couch. She leans forward on folded arms, holds
her head in her hands & covers her face.

(Like a bird, & not the feather.)

DOCTRINE CONNECTS ABOVE & BELOW
THE HIEROPHANT

   (What

would God say. Name the parts.
Define each name. His choice seen as emerging
from the dark side of reason

like a red Planet—

PARTY OF THE FLAME
FIVE OF WANDS

In the creamy white jag there are two witnesses.

Liberty walks smack
against the car & doesn't scream. Superimposed:
on headlights.

She is paralyzed; beautiful; accurate.
Her red skirt slides up her thighs, her mouth falls open.

She flips over twice, rights herself, skids back
on the macadam, breathes. Oxygen & hydrogen swerve
around her like a parlor trick.

An injured blue jay drags itself to the sidewalk.

Stand. Back & wait for the ricochet.

SWIFT LEAF WISH
SIX OF SWORDS

There's no doubt about it: the best
of what takes place between two people always
escapes them.

Just listen: I was there.

I remember birdsong & her beautiful, butchered
reflection, towering almost out of gunshot the trees eating
sun—

The burnt grasses part. God emerges.
She is ahead of him, combing earth from her hair.

Already, she is pure metaphor: muse
to Apollo, killed by Orpheus.

PARTY OF THE CRYSTAL
SIX OF PENTACLES

For your sake you say

surely you say *it is all wrong*—

The amusement park is hot & breathless, under a sky the green of unripe peaches.

You are stubbing your cigarette in a coffee cup.

You are saying *you didn't*.

(& Liberty being wind answers nothing.)

You didn't.

(After all whether suicide succeeds

or not isn't it still gathering her courage

a myth apparently based on accident, chance & unforeseeable distortion.)

PARTING WITH THE LOWER CASE
SIX OF WANDS, REVERSED

A paperscrap wobbles on the windowsill. You cut
& paste: bones swords spiders.

Black butterflies shift & flap. Meanwhile
on the television there are girl guides, dying baby

turtles, tarantulas in harness, a fleet of ships, miniature
horses & Vietnamese potbellied pigs.

A semi rumbles towards the Midwestern plains.
Flames stream across the screen like hair...

(Do you want to believe she wanted to live?) (Did
you want her to survive?

ALWAYS A VERB OR AT LEAST A GERUND
SIX OF CUPS

You drive past a gas station by the hospital & a radio
blaring a gospel show. Bare fields purple billboards & haunted
dead trees.

Here on the edge of town a sparrow is lodged
in an abandoned television & in both directions the road
thins & parts.

The stars make no sense at all. You are bitterly cold:
everywhere.

A deer flickers & is gone. A stroke of lightning rubs
the sunset.

Not unlike the amoeba, who live forever, her death is colloidal,
suspended:

but what but what but   *what*

You downshift, motor shrapnel skitters the highway
skyward. Crows fly from the eye, exit the canvas where you placed
her—

Spread out before you you know love's end before you have
remembered even the beginning: like

the shadow of a tree housing the soul of a nymph

THE USUAL FUTURE TENSE... IS HUNG
THE SUN, REVERSED

Admit it: you would not marry her.
It is guaranteed.

Her ghost? Is you misspelling
your own name, the sun shining in the wrong

part of the sky, wheat rotting under
a foot of floodwater.

You draw sooty diamonds,
a cemetery as seen from the top of a tree,

butterflies dissolving in exhaust,
cattle kneeling in green earth. You are drunk

& hungry & in the unanswerable
logic of nightmare

you hardly need exist. (I tell you:
there are no more windows & the truth

is passing between worlds hurts.

HUMAN ANATOMY
NINE OF PENTACLES, REVERSED

Pouring the sky like milk through her ribs.

Imagine: under what means in the heaven of having
lived Liberty sprawled in street shine grown

fleshly. Curling up inside what hidden dimension.

Birds plummet past matchstick trees.
Automobiles rusting, lopsided barns.

A cheerleader pops drunken wheelies in a cornfield.

You drive past a retrofitted three-story
farmhouse striped with the roots of trees. Who

can you turn to? Not God not Liberty not the girlfriend
who suspect you are already plurally someone

else. Imagine the mess. The sack of the heart. My
god: you need each other.

You are passing through that doorway, you
are turning the corner but the wind is strong & her

death has been with you since the beginning—

R IS FOR RECREATIONAL/REVELATIONAL
KING OF SWORDS

My God Liberty thinks, *how do normal
people deal with the mistakes they've made.* She is running
with a runner's ripe heat, shedding skins

of herself like the frames of a film. Here
on the edge of town where a bird nest is lodged
in an abandoned television & in both

directions the road thins
& parts, she begins to see the world
from above & to the right, as only

another could—or God. There are dogwoods
& fireflies, that hold a tinge of spring &
seem painful because they might vanish.

A blind woman eats watermelon. Other
people walk around, close to the trees. Wheat
rots under half a foot of floodwater.

Liberty turns her head & can't see any children—
& yet she knows there are birds—&
can't hear them either. A satellite blinks: in beautiful

equation. (*Auto da fe*. Is it you

"SPIRITUAL EXERCISES"
TEN OF PENTACLES, REVERSED

You drive through radar, drive
through radio waves, past stunted stippo, asphalt,
howling molecules, the story

you do not live that comes while
you are reconciling &

vanishes. You pass a half-flooded softball field,
turn onto unpainted blacktop.

Cardinals leap through leaf
vault. You eat aspirin, consider a cigarette.

Stars gather, gutter, come out
in angels & reality signs. You are starting
to think of it

as the affair & it comes to stand
for everything: loving at breakneck & getting
nowhere, feeling crimsoneyed

& drunk & abused, passionate
& useless, her legs about your buttocks &
your elbows keeping silence on

her ribs. (After all it's the same world
whether she lives or dies but not if you, whoever

you are, do—

ACROBATS OF THE PSYCHIC MISDEMEANOR

ONE

When you are a suicide, there is no one to love you, not even your own self.

TWO

Name Your Bird Without A Gun was conceived from the shame of having the kind of secret people just don't tell, and the moral dilemma of lying about your own self, out of etiquette.

THREE

The first time I intentionally overdose I am on my honeymoon in Vancouver, almost exactly one year after I eloped in the Black Mountain woods where, amongst other things, Charles Olson, Robert Creeley, and Robert Duncan once promoted "projective verse."
    I am Midwestern and embarrassed; I don't know how to help myself, whether I want to help myself, and I do everything *not* to survive: I argue with my young, desperate husband about calling the ambulance, I insist I don't need to go to the emergency room, and I end up phoning my father, the family physician, who will tell me what is real, if I'm ok. When my mother answers the phone, I can't, I would *die* rather than tell her.

FOUR

Vancouver is erupting with Chinese fireworks.
    I am young and in love. It is still possible to confuse this suicide attempt with romance. To believe I can turn the shock of becoming *the sort of person who* into something beautiful.
    But the brutal reality is I am capable of taking my own life.
    I write about *a dream of distance/ in which the husband can be/ both far from/ & near to* and a woman *not considering herself a special receptacle/ for eggs,* about drawing a door (about the size and shape of a sparrow) only I can pass through.
    I refer to myself in the second person, then the third. *There is,* I write, *no way of saying yes/ again, no way to disappear get out/ of the way, succumb.*

FIVE

Fate bestows me an Immortal Beloved: bestow, as in "devote to" or "impart gratuitously"— done freely, and without reason—and "Immortal Beloved," as in a paramour I desire but can never be with. Like Beethoven's Immortal Beloved, he is absent, ideal, imaginary, and sparks a crisis both creative and personal. Shocked by what I am capable of, my faithlessness, I run away with my cat to Florida, where I can procrastinate on getting on with my life, where I have no one to answer to and I can be anyone—married, divorced, in love with the dream of a lover whose life will never fully intersect with mine, who will never uncover the truth beneath my lies, for whom I will never be forced to pretend I am *sane, responsible, reliable*.

~

A girlfriend from North Carolina visits. She brings marijuana, Tarot, Elvis magnets, an unpainted potted owl. We get up before dawn, drink strong, black coffee, smoke the marijuana out of a glass pipe shaped like a dragon, and talk feminism, the forgotten Mississippi poet besmilr brigham, and the sexual politics of meat. When we tire of theory, we walk to a dive bar and talk Tarot over blonde beers and strawberries—how the cards might belong to the sacred myths of gypsies or Thoth or Dionysus or Pythagoras or even aliens. We like the cards because they are *liberated* from time, geography, and spiritual tradition. Working with them requires what we are so desperate to do, what we will never, as writers, quite accomplish: *letting go of intent*.

SIX

I want to capture the moment of transgression and hold it there, suspended, in all of its horrible potential. Before there can be forgiveness, before there can be remorse.

SEVEN

All that summer I make lists, I try out forms, I diagram choice.

<u>Suicide</u>
problem-solving behavior
closed world with its own irresistible logic
unanswerable logic of nightmare
superstitious, and full of omens
like being in love (Freud)
ego overwhelmed by object
ambitious act
insidious vocation
prepared within the silence of the heart
some suicides are born, not made

<u>A. Alvarez, *The Savage God: A Study of Suicide*</u>

Homer records self-murder without comment, as something natural and usually heroic.

Poe and Berlioz swallowed near lethal doses of opium during the course of unhappy love affairs, and, instead of dying, were inspired. (As in liberated—to do, to make, to write.)

Animal suicide is a manifestation of intelligence.

Like divorce, suicide is a confession of failure. And like divorce, it is shrouded in excuses and rationalizations spun endlessly to disguise the simple fact. Those who survive suicide survive into a changed life…

The theorists help untangle the intricacy of motive and define the deep ambiguity of the wish to die but they say little about what it means to be suicidal, and how it feels.

<u>Sexual Phases from Immortality</u>
period of athletic muteness
period of metaphors
period of obscene truth
period of telephone
mystical period

<u>Reverse Ekphrasis</u>
cradle
path
the burning book
puppet
window
garland of fruit
rider
staff

~

I promise myself I will not cheat on the husband again but find myself fucking another man the same day I arrive in France, where, it is said, the separation of love and eroticism gives the populace access to both. I visit the Chateau de Villandry, with gardens like mazes, mazes fashioned from the rhetoric of love, the rhetoric of love like instructions for an affair. It is an intentional structure with enough flexibility to accommodate the personal, as proposing an emotional world, a work in movement.

<u>The French Renaissance Rhetoric of Love</u>

Tender: Voluptuous shapes in domino masks in the center of the hedges and flames of love in the form of flowers in the corners symbolize union.

Passionate: The boxed hedges that crisscross to form a maze are said to represent love broken apart by passion.

Fickle: Four fans in the corners symbolize the volatile nature of feelings. Between the fans, there are the horns of the jilted lover, who, fantastically, is almost always the man. In the center yellow (the color of jilted love) flowers represent the billets doux the fickle lady sends her new lover.

Tragic: The shapes of the flowers depict the blades of daggers and swords used during the duel provoked by the lovers' rivalry. In the summer, flowers bloom red from the center to symbolize blood spilt as love turns tragic.

I put my heroine in that situation, a terrible present in which she grieves the sudden death of her young husband, falls in love—or so she thinks—with a lyric womanizer, and, upon learning she has unwittingly become The Mistress and finding herself nonetheless incapable of leaving him, commits suicide.

EIGHT

They say that *every Tarot reading is an act of psychic improvisation to which there are at least two sides: heimarmene, the compulsion of the stars which is not irrevocable and can be altered with sufficient consciousness; and moira, one's portion, one's allotment, to which even the gods are subject. The distinction between the two, and the fact that in a given situation we never know whether we are dealing with heimarmene or moira, means we have to go with the assumption it's the former.*

Heimarmene: that which we are *liberated to.*

Moira: that which we must be *freed from.*

The assumption: we have to go with liberty.

As an adulteress and a suicide, I find the proposition troublesome.

In the margins in sea-faded Sharpie I write: *my marriage failed because I lacked the freedom to be myself.* Upon re-reading this statement years later, after I have finally found the courage to divorce my husband, I cross out *freedom* and add *first*.

NINE

I name the heroine of *Name Your Bird Without A Gun* Liberty and I come to think of her as a woman, and as an ideal.

Liberty, I learn, was a fundamental American value for the nation's founders and was [as opposed to freedom] the dominant patriotic theme in the young nation's first one-hundred-and-fifty years. Liberty has since receded from our vocabulary and been replaced with freedom, a virtue referring to economic enterprise, religion, speech, the press and/or private property.

Grammatically, we are freed *from* something, like want or fear. Freedom *excludes* and *prohibits*, whereas we are liberated *to do* something—for example, pursue happiness.

The history of liberty, Woodrow Wilson writes, *is the history of resistance.*

If liberty means anything at all, George Orwell argues, *it means the right to tell people what they do not want to hear.*

Liberty, George Bernard Shaw cautions, *means responsibility. This is why most men dread it.*

TEN

When I OD for the second time I am living in Oregon, my lover is angry and doesn't take me to the hospital and, because I am afraid of him, I don't insist. It's quite literally a miracle I am alive and my liver is still functioning.

I don't learn anything from the second attempt, I can't make it beautiful, and I feel desperate, and out of control.

ELEVEN

I write *Name Your Bird Without A Gun* in Orlando; Johnson, Vermont; in Amsterdam; in Montreal; in Calgary; in Orlando; in Santa Cruz; in Missouri; in Oregon; at a winery in Sonoma, California. In 2010, 2012, 2014, 2017, and 2019.

TWELVE

What I need is not a narrative but a form of listening: a structure with enough resilience to accommodate the ways our lives misstep, mistake.

THIRTEEN

I fly home on Christmas Day, my mother's birthday. This is rare, and a cause for celebration. My parents drive to the city. We drink French wine and eat lobster and cheesecake with a view of the St. Louis Arch. Though my father is a medical school dean, my immaculate Midwestern parents budget for a junior hotel suite. I sleep on the couch and when I am startled awake before dawn, my mother is sitting at my feet, in pajamas and her Walmart reading glasses.

My youngest sister has just phoned our father from the Raleigh-Durham airport to say she has been dreading this Christmas. Though no one knew about the sexual abuse at the time, she can't forgive our mother for inviting our crazy uncle to her wedding, and she isn't getting on the plane.

~

My mother navigates the cold, empty streets of downtown St. Louis with a desperate imprecision. She weaves over yellow lines and jams on the brake at stop signs.

I worry, my mother says, *that she's going to hurt herself.*

I don't, I say without thinking, *think she's that kind of person.*

It's not until the words are leaving my mouth that I realize what I am saying is that I am that kind of person. That there is that kind of person.

If you ever, my mother says, *try that again I'll haunt you in your grave. So now,* I say, *you're threatening me?*

Then I laugh, non-ironically. In all of my life that I can remember, my mother has only hugged me once, after my first suicide. Nonetheless, I know I am—and have always been—loved.

We are hardwired to be perfectionists, my mother and I, and, in this moment, it feels possible to be broken together, to admit we are broken, together.

~

The Whole Foods is as deserted and as disorienting as the streets of downtown St. Louis: brightly-lit and hopeful, full of suburban holiday cheer,. At the checkout there are what I assume to be parmesan cheese samples. As my mother mouths *STOP* over my left shoulder, I wash out my own mouth with a wavy yellow disk that turns out to be artisanal soap.

Then, as immaculate Midwesterners, we get back in the minivan, we keep driving, and we do not talk anymore about the suicides or the sister who won't come home.

FOURTEEN

After the second time I OD, a kind but confused and likely desperate friend mails me a random assortment of second-hand stuffed animals: a talking gorilla, a tiger in a top hat, a bear with a blank stare, a blue flamingo, an enormous, exuberantly-colored parrot fish. I keep the animals on display on my bedroom dresser—as inanimate guardians, talismans that I am loved, that I can be beloved, symbols of all the strange places the heart ends up.

~

Mostly unsuccessfully, the heart tries out affairs with built-in expiration dates: with an Iranian-Canadian digital artist, a sociopathic software engineer, an alcoholic carpenter, a tuba-playing pathologist, a young Norwegian plumber. When the pathologist spends asks about the stuffed animals, my explanation is brief, honest, unapologetic. He is clinical and bald, like a soft mole bewildered in disclosure's harsh light. *Thank you*, he says, *it's brave of you to share that*. Or *thank you*, he says, *for your self-awareness*. Or *thank you*, he says, *it's over, then*. They always want to know that *it's over, then*—as if you could selectively self-lobotomize the part of yourself that wants to die.

FIFTEEN

In her homage to the "suicidal genius" Thomas James, Lucie Brock-Broido writes that, *according to Lorca, when the Angel sees death on the way, he flies in slow circles and weaves tears of narcissus and ice. When the Muse sees death, she closes the door. But the Duende will not approach at all if he does not see the possibility of death. Lorca writes: Everywhere else, death is an end. Death's possibility— the necessity of its proximity—is that which makes art human and alive.*

SIXTEEN

I adopt a street dog from Guadalajara. In addition to the dimensions of my backyard and philosophy on discipline and training, the application involves responding to a series of scenarios in which I have to give up Frito for unforeseen emergencies, incompatibility, and/or my sudden demise. I answer correctly, and my skinny, scared puppy arrives just in time for Memorial Day.

Though the Collie in his face and the Jack Russell in his build make Frito look mischievous and up-for-anything—the little dog at the heels of the Tarot's proverbial Fool—his personality is trapped inside his fear, and he doesn't know how to live inside love.

It breaks my heart.

I try to train him to trust the world.

The paradox of this pursuit is equal parts tender and terrifying. We visit a popular local bakery and stand in a line that wraps around the brick building twice. The puppyish charm and cute black and brown mask on his muzzle inspire sticky-handed children and happy-eyed young women to swarm at him with outstretched arms. He tucks his tail between his legs, runs behind me, and tries to disappear.

He's shy, I explain. *Please don't try to pet him.*

When I tie him up by the door, I tell him *I'll be right back, it's okay, I love you.*

I wait in line inside and peek anxiously over my shoulder and out the window. A grandmother and her pre-teen granddaughter offer to wait outside with the dog. A middle-aged woman in front of me suggests I bring a toy next time.

That way, she says, *he knows you're coming back. Take him shopping,* she advises, *and let him choose the toy.*

I thank her and joke about how he's made the wrong choice, opting for me in a world full of sadness and sharp edges.

Perhaps, she says, *that's because you both fear the world.* She turns around and orders some jalapeño ham croissants.

SEVENTEEN

I dream Frito is attacked by a pit bull. The dog attacks once, twice, the third time goes for the jugular in slomotion. Frito yelps, tries to free himself. I watch, helpless.

The conventional interpretation of this kind of dream is 1) inner conflict and/or 2) someone is being disloyal and trying to betray you.

~

The dedication to my third book reads *there is no story in which my failure to love my husband is not background.* In retrospect, the failure to love the husband is perhaps merely a symptom of the underlying disease, which involves my remarkable ability to betray my own self. I used to believe this quality was what made the art so beautiful and alive.

~

Etymologically, "acrobat" is associated with harlequin clowns and tightrope acts. "Misdemeanor" can refer to a crime without intent—in this case possibly not identified as a crime at all, or misidentified as such, buried as it is in the psyche. For some: a sin.

~

Shame and mercy, Anne Carson writes—*people who lack one lack the other.*

EIGHTEEN

Life goes on, goes upside down, inside-out, sideways, rights itself somewhere left of center and starts over.

The Immortal Beloved finds a job building Lego sculptures and settles in the Bronx with his Dutch-Korean wife and their three-year-old son. He persists in my memory not as a man, but the idea of a man—like the Tarot's Hanged Man, a magic eight ball saying *not yet, try again later.*

My mother texts every morning: to remind me I'm loved, or to confirm I'm alive, or possibly both. After reading some excerpts from *Name Your Bird Without A Gun* online, she writes: "Unsettling. Is this you?"

"Not me," I respond, "fiction."

"Relief," she writes. "Tough poems. Good writing. Another storm coming this weekend with lows in the teens."

My cat of fifteen years, who—though mostly absent from this account—has been the one constant throughout, dies suddenly of a feline aortic thromboembolism (FATE) and I face the prospect of starting over without her for the first time in my adult life. This is how I come to learn my ex-husband is semi-incarcerated by his family in an Orlando suburb due to two sincere suicide attempts.

After flirting with death for a third time, I've just accepted a teaching position at a liberal arts college in Florida and in two months I'll be living less than an hour from where my ex is recovering from his mistakes. Part of me knows I can't ignore my culpability and the other part of me knows the worst thing I could do—for him, for me, for *us*—is try to take responsibility.

NINETEEN

The Tarot's major Arcana is said to depict the soul's journey from the conscious (the outer self) through the subconscious (the inner self) to the superconscious (the negotiation between the outer and inner selves), ending with Judgment and the World and then starting over with the conscious. It's a journey that never ends; you finish in order to begin again.

Judgment is the card of criticism and conscience, reconciliation and resurrection, when the dead speak to their living. EVERYTHING must be accounted for—particularly your evasions and self- betrayals. You will be tempted towards either narcissism (no accountability) or self-recrimination (total accountability); both are ego-driven and will prevent you from achieving the Total Integration the World requires.

Some Tarot readers try to simplify the World to harmony and/or balance—illusions as dangerous as our obsession with self-help, or that peculiar narrative of adults as Survivors. When in reality the World isn't a solution so much as a distillation: who you are   have always been—essentially.

Death-driven, and full of indecision.

TWENTY

My story—Liberty's story—is, in the end, not so different from yours. The moral—if there is one to be had—involves not, as the talk shows or the celebrity pundits would have it, freedom from judgment but rather the liberty to love ourselves, as we really are.

POST SCRIPT

According to legend, on her first day at Harvard Jorie Graham told her students: *writing poems helps us go through something we might otherwise choose to go around. And so the decision to write poems is the decision to live inside one's difficulties, to inhabit them, to trespass against the solitudes they wish to keep… poetry tracks the life of the soul while that other, louder life goes on—the domestic life, our illnesses and work, our car accidents and lonesome subway rides. If you look back on what you've written, you'll read the words of that secret, soulful life, of what was really going on.*

~

You've been put on this Earth and there is no blueprint, no instruction, no guidebook. By definition there is no master scheme. Life can only be an experiment and we are neither the sole authors nor incapable of authoring.

       Mistakes were made. Mistakes will be made. Some days the creek goes underground, and you can't stop it. The question isn't how to get better [you won't] but how to live well within chaos and/or urgency.

~

I said to a friend, Clarise Lispector once wrote in her mini crónica "Yes," *life always asked too much of me.*
       She replied but don't forget you also ask too much of life.

CYCLOPEDIA OF CARD MEANINGS

SUITS

Cups persuade, & are tender.
Wands compete, & are passionate.
Swords rescue, & are fickle.
Pentacles possess, & are tragic.

MINOR ARCANA

Aces require courage.
Twos require balance.
Threes require foresight.
Fours require organization.
Fives require a new approach.
Sixes require recollection.
Sevens require decision.
Eights require letting go.
Nines require self-reliance.
Tens require closure.

THE COURT CARDS, ON A GOOD DAY

Pages bring messages.
Knights have a mission.
Queens use their feelings usefully.
Kings philosophize.

MAJOR ARCANA

Fools begin.
Magicians make.
High Priestesses keep secrets.
Empresses give birth.
Emperors lead coups d'état.
Hierophants conform.
Lovers make choices.
Chariots are victorious.
Strength acts with compassion.
Hermits turn inward.
Wheels of Fortune are in flux.
Justice seeks equilibrium.
Hanged Men make prophecies.
Deaths are transformative.
Temperance is in excess.
Devils tempt.
Towers are catastrophic.
Stars have visions.
Moons reflect.
Suns orientate.
Judgements reckon.
Worlds consummate.

INDEX OF KEY WORDS

MINOR ARCANA

CUPS

Ace of Cups Reversed | scarcity, rejection, promiscuity | pg 6
by believing you lacked a desire to know

Two of Cups Reversed | misunderstanding, unbalance, discord | pg 7
why not why. tell the truth or I'll jump

Three of Cups Reversed | there's more to the story & it's not necessarily happy news | pg 76
the truth is: there are three exits (more   than enough

Four of Cups | trying to understand the self | pg 77
when you are human & alone—

Five of Cups | mourning, regrets, resurrection | pg 10
show me

Six of Cups | the past is becoming the present | pg 84
like the shadow of a tree housing the soul of a nymph

Seven of Cups | temptation, a crossroads, superficial love | pg 17
get out of my dream get   out

Eight of Cups Reversed | homelessness, literally or spiritually | pg 37
when people are ready to, they change. sometimes they die before they can get around to it

Nine of Cups | wishful thinking | pg 44
is it you or is it us

Ten of Cups | ultimate happiness; balance between heaven & earth | pg 24
you were there, you ought to know

WANDS

Ace of Wands | initial attraction | pg 28
Madame Bovary sitting down with a pen & the notion of Flaubert, c'est moi

Two of Wands | a fate in which you have confidence | pg 33
there is no death like this except (if you remember it) your baptism

Three of Wands | one step short of success; cooperation is needed | pg 35
a terror in which you have confidence

Four of Wands Reversed | compromise, lack of appreciation, discord | pg 11
another dumb animal making that final leap—

Five of Wands | third-party interference | pg 80
stand. back & wait for the ricochet

Six of Wands Reversed | postponement | pg 83
(did you want to survive?

Seven of Wands | backed into a corner & standing your ground | pg 36
the terrifying thing is that it is done—not what   you've done but that it is over

Eight of Wands Reversed | look before you leap | pg 19
like Midas touching his daughter, roses, servants, the water in a fountain

Nine of Wands Reversed | let go & take the offensive | pg 41
what do you want you ought to make up your mind

Ten of Wands | too many responsibilities; everyday life; other people's burdens | pg 46
this would make a good ending, you think. but you go on living of course

SWORDS

Ace of Swords Reversed | entropy, chaos & short-lived victory | pg 50
*alone with your conscience, playing a complex game of proximity &
distance*

Two of Swords | stalemate, a Catch-22 | pg 74
you know what I'm saying. somehow you should let her go—

Three of Swords | heartbreak because you have a heart | pg 52
which is more demanding—deception of others or self-deception

Four of Swords | a literal or figurative retreat | pg 53
what sacrifice: is necessary in the endeavor to become yourself

Five of Swords | empty victory, lies for personal gain | pg 54
*is it that we aspire to forget the stories we already know. or do we learn
to forget*

Six of Swords | running away from the past, & carrying all those old
burdens along | pg 81
pure metaphor: muse to Apollo, killed by Orpheus

Seven of Swords | trust issues, white lies, disregard for consequences
| pg 55
someone   was going to get hurt—

Eight of Swords | a false sense of victimhood | pg 60
well for one thing who really was the victim here—

Nine of Swords | a matter "written in the stars" | pg 65
the question isn't how to get better [you won't]

Ten of Swords Reversed | move on on your own & don't look back |
pg 68
think of better outcomes. be specific. how so

111

PENTACLES

Ace of Pentacles Reversed | a false sense of security | pg 72
because of future possibility. or because. there is no cause

Two of Pentacles Reversed | juggling too many responsibilities | pg 51
did you think it's be waltz come let's   waltz

Three of Pentacles | validation, rewards | pg 34
one wants to create a bright new future. why shouldn't you

Four of Pentacles | the miser card | pg 78
a page straight from God's book

Five of Pentacles | delusion, codependency, divine intervention | pg 10
the lie all lovers tell themselves: we invented this

Six of Pentacles | wearing your heart on your sleeve | pg 82
a myth apparently based on accident, change & unforeseeable distortion

Seven of Pentacles | diligence, hard work, & attention to detail | pg 16
there is no story in which your failure is not background—

Eight of Pentacles | diligence, hard work & attention to detail | pg 86
everybody seems ok with that bargain

Nine of Pentacles Reversed | dissatisfaction; more effort than recognition | pg 88
imagine the mess. the sack of the heart

Ten of Pentacles Reversed | retreat, dissolution, the end | pg 84
the story you do not live that comes while you are reconciling & vanishes

COURT CARDS

CUPS

Page of Cups | a prophecy; fact versus truth | pg 8
it's because I love you that your death has set me free

Knight of Cups | emotions escalate; criticism; self-doubt | pg 89
fate. which requires less than volition. it requires only inertia

Queen of Cups | activity feeds the dream | pg 20
it's just a memory you can chance it

King of Cups | Charlemagne, or a troubled conscience | pg 21
in the delirium of a summer afternoon. the affair begins.

WANDS

Page of Wands | confidence, & lots of youth | pg 29
nothing but nothing could have stopped you

Knight of Wands Reversed | second-guessing yourself | pg 63
every story has a tense; it must take place in time

Queen of Wands Reversed | capitulation, surrender, sacrifice | pg 39
in honor of a beauty that owes us nothing

King of Wands | quick to temper, quick to judgment | pg 42
after this, a happy ending seems unnecessary—

SWORDS

Page of Swords | adversity versus opportunity | pg 56
there is no simple way to confront the persons you are not...

Knight of Swords | not intellect but courage, the very model of a knight | pg 62
the past is redeemed, you are forgiven—

Queen of Swords | soul & butterfly; a woman who knows sorrow | pg 73
the desire was there all along it is born not made

King of Swords | metamorphosis, controversy | pg 87
how do normal people deal with the mistakes they've made

PENTACLES

Page of Pentacles Reversed | waste; excess; artifice | pg 61
for how much of your life have you regretted the decisions that saved you

Knight of Pentacles Reversed | inertia, standstill, lack of courage | pg 66
you've come this far so why not—

Queen of Pentacles Reversed | vanity, vulnerability, dependence | pg 14
not a life already lived so much as a life that stopped moving forward into the past

King of Pentacles | forging alliances; competition | pg 23
everyone's love has a problem what's   yours

MAJOR ARCANA

The Fool | a honeymoon period, don't get swept away | pg 27
I can't say for sure I'll always

The Magician | Newton's first law of motion | pg 40
this heartbreaking beauty, the saving core of reality, that will go on, when there is no heart left to break for it—

The High Priestess Reversed | secrets, hypocrisy, broken intuition | pg 32
it is not like fate but rather as if reality had disappeared

The Empress | unintended or unanticipated consequences | pg 67
how any story is finally about the lengths the mind will carry it to, to explain what the body already knows

The Emperor | jus ad bellum | pg 22
do not be embarrassed. do not skip the difficult parts. do not be embarrassed

The Hierophant | good intentions gone wrong; group-think; what society deems "right" | pg 79
name the parts. define each name

The Lovers | beware of first impressions | pg 30
in retrospect, you can: forgive yourself for everything—

The Chariot Reversed | make better choices | pg 71
you are not sorry that is someone you never learned how to be

Strength Reversed | action | pg 57
between you you know there is something more than love: complicity

The Hermit Reversed | learn from others rather than your own mistakes | pg 38
is this normal. there's no way   to tell

The Wheel of Fortune Reversed | turning point, an "act of god," going against the current | pg 64
like the desert wolf who lost his wife & went to the land of the dead for her

Justice | Newton's third law of motion | pg 43
she will rise from the earth like an animal & she will go—

Hanged Man Reversed | self-obsession & martyrdom | pg 59
it's a new day full of promises you can't keep, or are choosing not be able…

Death Reversed | inertia, mortality, suffering | pg 12
I am only   my mother

Temperance | inner balance; action without ego; opposites attract | pg 18
go on: finish those years that might have belonged   to someone else

The Devil | virtue abandoned & desire indulged | pg 31
the tacit agreement you made from the start. it keeps its word

The Tower | hubris & catastrophe | pg 49
the world sees you for what you are without   my help

The Star Reversed | hopelessness, self-doubt, depression | pg 75
where even the brave—how would you say—have no windows

The Moon Reversed | "everything that rises must converge" | pg 13
she is the heroine let her do it—

The Sun Reversed | negligence, lethargy, a warning | pg 85
there are not more windows & the truth is passing between worlds hurts

Judgment Reversed | misinterpretation & misreckoning | pg 45
you had to do it—you had no idea why

The World Reversed | denial, ambiguity, willful ignorance | pg 5
what happened versus sometimes what it meant

ACKNOWLEDGMENTS

Excerpts from Name Your Bird Without A Gun were published in chapbook form by Tarpaulin Sky, dancing girl press, and the *Fairy Tale Review*. Individual cards were published in *witchcraft magazine, A Bad Penny Review, Posit, Front Porch, Hayden's Ferry Review, Peacock, Alice Blue, web Conjunctions, New Limestone Review*, the *Notre Dame Review*, and *Blackbox Manifold*. An earlier version of "Acrobats of the Psychic Misdemeanor" was published in the Operating System's Field Notes series.

REFERENCES

While writing this book, I relied on Rachel K Pollack's and Benebell Wen's Tarot handbooks and Mary K. Greer's Tarot blog.

Quotes have been borrowed from the following authors:

Jane Bowles: *The terrifying thing is that is it done—not what you've done but that it is over*

Louise Glück: *even this will be taken from her, as all lies are.*

Erin Moure: *Lord it is so easy: to say someone loved you. Pawned himself, limb after. Pulled his spent pronoun through. Light, at his back.*

Flannery O'Connor: *Everything that rises must converge.*

Rainer Maria Rilke: *Love is a terror whose outcome we don't fear… A terror in which we have confidence.*

Andy Warhol: *When people are ready to, they change. Sometimes they die before they can get around to it.*

Joy Williams: *She is reading the lives of saints: dying men pierced by arrows & women staring at the white leopards of heaven as flames lick their breasts. She likes the ornately lettered names, the early paragraphs yawning with martyrs, waiting to be tempted.*

… this heartbreaking beauty, the saving core of reality, that will go on, when there is no heart left to break for it.

… girl guides, dying baby turtles, tarantulas in harness, a fleet of ships, miniature horses & Vietnamese potbellied pigs…

C.D. Wright: *Think of better outcomes. Be specific. How so.*

The desire was there all along it is born not made.

AUTHOR BIOGRAPHY

Emily Carr writes murder mysteries that turn into love poems that are sometimes called divorce poems. She's passionate about the rediscovery of Mississippi poet besmilr brigham, the sexual politics of meat, the limits of Achilles' honesty and the problem of Chaucer's spring, un-posted love letters, cannibal chickens and a ship too late to save the drowning witch. These days, she's Visiting Assistant Professor of Creative Writing at the New College of Florida. *Name Your Bird Without A Gun: a Tarot romance* is Emily's fourth book. Her third collection of poetry, *whosoever has let a minotaur enter them, or a sonnet—*, is available from McSweeney's. It inspired a beer of the same name, now available at the Ale Apothecary. Visit Emily online at www.ifshedrawsadoor.com or on Instagram as ifshedrawsadoor.

CPSIA information can be obtained
at www.ICGtesting.com
Printed in the USA
JSHW042017240420
5287JS00001B/31